The Em

of

My Condition

Poems by

David Sharif

ISBN: 978-1-6780-8886-6

Acknowledgements

The first person to thank is my grandmother Myra Shapiro who read these poems, talked with me about them, and made suggestions. On top of that, how she enriched poetry to our friends and family.

My parents, Karen Shapiro and Syud Sharif who have strived relentlessly for my future education, let me enroll in any kind of activity I wanted.

My brother Benjamin Sharif for giving me the idea to pursue similar things that he did without me. Moreover, teaching me how to read tricky and catchable ironic sentences.

A major shout out to all of the hard-working instructors, well-trained coaches and therapists from my schooling.

The numerous counselors and directors I have come in contact with from the organizations that have become a strong influence on my success.

Last but not least, to everyone in the Shapiro/Sharif family tree, along with my universal comrades.

Contents

For my grandparents who laid the groundwork for every fortune.

Nasima Sharif (1928 - 2001)

Mohammed Sharif Bhatti (1924 - 2016)

Harold Shapiro (1927 - 2017)

"Autism can't define me. I define autism."

– Kerry Magro

"Everyone has a mountain to climb and autism has not been my mountain, it has been my opportunity for victory."

- Rachel Barcellona

"I am different, not less."

- Temple Grandin

Autism Diagnosis

My behavior changed rapidly
I was different
My parents knew that I have autism
I lashed out
When things didn't go as planned

I discovered my senses were different
Covered my ears in large crowds
Irritated when people laughed at me
Banged my head when I lost

I was evaluated by pediatricians
Communicating verbally was a success
Expressing myself accurately and
Making friends was the nuance

From a great deal of research
Enrolled in a multi-disciplinary school
Met with diverse pathologists and therapists
Pulled out of the classroom for meetings

Speech therapy to practice conversations

Behavioral therapy to manage my feelings

Drama therapy to know the audience is cackling at the act

Occupational therapy to build skills for daily activities

Went on field trips

Played games with my peers

Practiced idioms and unclear phrases

Learned to recognize sarcastic statements

My life became more general

Collaboration

Christopher Mulligan
A licensed clinical social worker
Leads group sessions every week
Hosts movie nights once a month

With him I
Shared my life updates
Played group games, **Apples to Apples, Black Jack**
Expressed my opinions on films, *To Kill A Mockingbird, Kingpin*

With him I
Attended a filming day camp
Was recorded on camera acting out scenes
From *Goonies and Frankenstein*
Watched hilarious scenes from movies released in the 1990s

Mulligan, the humorous critical thinker
Let me sit comfortably on beanbags
Taught me adaptation skills with wagering and violence
Tested my knowledge on a quiz game app

Dog Love

My friend lives in a gorgeous apartment
Close to Venice Beach
She has a black and white Havanese
Named Mr. Big

I
Had to learn the nature of dogs
How they are different from me
The way they talk
The way they listen
The way they touch

The dog
Barked at me non-stop when I entered
Came up to me while I was eating
Grumped at me when I said no
I called my friend for assistance
Put the dog in his crate for misbehavior

We
Took him for a walk by the rivers in Marina Del Rey
Played fetch on the sandy beach

He

Cooperated with the leash

Cuddled with me on the porch and in bed

Observing the dog's character I acquired

Unconditional Love

Showing Compassion

Seeing his Kindness

Traveling as a family

Traveled all my life

Trips with my brother and parents were
The United Arab Emirates & Pakistan
Summer trips to Iceland, Malaysia, and Scandinavia

Trips with the family were
Six provinces in Canada
A vacation in Costa Rica

Ten **Ocean Cruises**
Three in the Caribbean and Central America
Two in Alaska and Glacier Bay
Two in Western Mexico
One in the Baltic and Mediterranean Seas
One in the New England Area
One in the Fjords, Arctic Circle, and United Kingdom
Three **River Cruises**
The Rhine River
The Seine River
The Douro River of Gold

Grateful to have shared marvelous places
With my brother, parents, and grandparents

We are Travel Comrades

- for Harrison

We met in first grade
Talked about airlines and car companies
Shared the places we've been too
Read atlases
Played with transportation toys

We attended religious school
Sat in the back of every classroom
Connected with peers who paved the way for loving sports
Obtained special appointments for Bar Mitzvah preparation

We went on weekend retreats and summer camp in Malibu
Slept on separate bunk beds
Climbed high ropes
Took walks with our counselor

We were at each other's Bar Mitzvahs
Opened the ark to introduce the Torah
Drank from a chocolate fountain
Had lots of ice cream

We remained in the same homeroom in high school
Persevered with mistreatment from some schoolmates
Traveled on every school world strides trip
Delivered our speeches at graduation

We departed on our post high school journeys
Phone called each other
Reflected on our togetherness
Said our favorite quote from The Simpsons: "We have a great life
here in Alaska and we ain't going back to America again."

Drama

Acted in a youth theatre program

Learned to play as part of the **ensemble**
Sang with a group of performers before transitioning to characters

Played **Augustus Gloop** in *Willy Wonka & the Chocolate Factory*
Chubby kid who eats too much

Played **Uncle Henry** and **A Lollipop Guild** in the *Wizard of Oz*
Wonderful and hardworking uncle of Dorothy Gale
Lovely munchkin who welcomes Dorothy Gale to Munchkin Land

Played **The King** in *Cinderella*
Strict, but caring and loyal father who is concerned about his son

Played **Freidrich** in *The Sound of Music*
Quiet and kind gentleman who describes himself 'impossible'

Played **Richard** in *Free to be you and me*
Ruthless kid who is reluctant to grow up and express himself

Played **Harvey Johnson** in *Bye Bye Birdie*
Fair average stereotypical teenager

Played **Big Jule** in *Guys and Dolls*
Sore loser and gambler who refuses to learn from his mistakes

Played **Jacob** in *Joseph and the Amazing Technicolor Dreamcoat*
Loving father who favors Joseph as his special son
Out of all twelve boys

Played **Yertle the Turtle** and **The Grinch** in *Seussical*
The King of the pond who leads Horton's trial
Notable resident of Whoville who arranges the Christmas Pageant

Played **Officer Ward** and **Drake** in *Annie*
Police officer who searches for Annie
Very mature and friendly adult who is the butler
At the Warbucks Mansion

Played **Cogsworth** in *Beauty and the Beast*
Serious-minded clock who follows the masters orders

Played **Fyedka** in *Fiddler on the Roof*
Charming Russian who embodies, passion, reading, and love

Played **Sonny** in *Grease*
Humorous dude who loves to joke around

Played **Brad, Mr. Spritzer**, and **A Security Guard** in *Hairspray*
Top performer on the Corny Collins show
Close-minded president of Ultra Clutch
Agent who makes informal decisions at the big-doll house

Every production a memory
Made wonderful friends

Music

Piano was the instrument
Played from ages seven to eighteen
Lessons begun with a teacher in Santa Monica
Continued with another instructor at my house

Pieces were from the
1800s to 2000s
Top favorite songs were
The NBA on TNT
The Beatles, John Williams, Disney, James Bond

Performed in eleven recitals: Two in school
Three at a piano center
Two at a public library
Three at my teacher's house
One at a luxury home

Piano
Decreased my anxiety
Kept my mind active
Increased my feeling for music

Intramurals

Picked up a basketball at the age of five
Dribbled and made shots in different spots
Shuffled my feet
Competed in a Recreational Youth League

Four seasons in the Little Leagues
Summer 2004, Winter 2005, Summer 2006, Winter 2007
Committed to developing my game

Contacted a coach
Monitored my movements
Ran on hills

Three seasons in the minors
Summer 2007, Winter and Summer 2008
Won first place in two summer seasons

At 11 played four seasons in the majors
Winter and Summer 2009, Winter and Summer 2010
Rebounded missed shots

Attended a boys day camp at LMU
Finished first place in a hot-shot contest
Swam in the campus pool

At 13 played three seasons in the juniors
Winter 2011, 2012, 2013
Concluded my final season with a first place victory

Played high school basketball
Was asked to join prior to my freshman year
Matched up with school staff and private schools in the LA area

Cherished the lessons
Knew my strengths and weaknesses
Strong shooter, weak rebounder
Significance of teamwork
Paid attention to details

Team Prime Time

Came across *The Prime Time Games*
An after school program
Offered to individuals at risk and special needs

Attended a sports day camp for four summers
Examined my physicality in the games
Soccer
My feet hurt after every kick
Flag Football
Couldn't run fast enough to the end zone
Dodge Ball
Caught balls thrown at me

Basketball
Shot more than forty consecutive free throws
Sat by myself to zero in
Spoke with the directors about my ambitions

Bonded with athletic staff
Ran through an aisle full of high fives
Gave brief messages to welcome participants

Commemorated eighteen seasons with medals
Met James Worthy and got his basketball
Treasured the philosophies

Results signify an accomplishment
Improving enhances your self-esteem
Knowing how you play counts the most

Ball Game

Grandpa was a Yankee
Mom is a Brave and Cub
I grew up a Dodger

Played second base and center field
For a team called Texas Rangers.
Kept score for my synagogues softball team
Called Boychicks

Begged mom to get Dodgers tickets every summer
In the upper decks behind home-plate
With dodger dogs, popcorn, and a helmet of fries

Learned the lessons
Be prepared for the unexpected
Accept Failure
Stay in the moment

Summer Camp: Six Summers

Embarked on a magical journey
Entered the gates of Camp Havaya
A summer camp in the Poconos

Took one day at a time
Delivered my autism speech
Boated in the lake and swam in the pool
Climbed tall trees
Zipped over the lake
Created artistic representations of
My favorite baseball logos and super heroes
Cooked flavorful desserts
Performed in the weekly talent show
Played sports and watched the Frisbee Tournament

Went on field trips
Hiked on rocky trails
Pontooned on heavy waves
Made smores
Rode fast coasters
Celebrated Shabbat
Chanted prayers and danced the hora

Adventured the Holy Land for a month
Studied the history of Judaism and cultural relations
Participated in a building and leadership program
Gave a talk: My connection to camp

Became a counselor
Earned my first paid job
Brought the joy of camp
As a staff member shared my autism story

Had the freedom to be myself
Played movie quoting games
Used my love for Harry Potter
Made everlasting friendships
Became a member of an extraordinary family

Long Life Best Friend
- *for Sam*

Ran into a handsome dude with a baseball cap
Life bestowed a remarkable gift
My long life best friend

Celebrated Birthdays
Traveled to Israel
Messaged each other after school
Built our home away from home
Became staff members at camp
Went on retreats
Took Shabbat photos
Visited our universities
Played chess
Bickered about sports and athletes
Discussed political outcomes

You taught me how to catch a Frisbee
You were on my back when I socially struggled
You sat close to me on every bus ride
You were ready for me to hug you
You motivated me to persevere with mistreatment
You were the one who told me to stay true to myself

You told me where to locate while climbing trees
You were kind when I misunderstood anything
You held my hand when I couldn't see a thing
You were there for me when I needed you most
You became my favorite man in the world

Our endless camaraderie went beyond inconceivable odds
We will always be together
Life is great when I vision you in my dreams

Strike

Bowling is a game
Allowing individuals
To perform individually
And as a team. As a boy
I practiced my arm swing
Out of the bowling alley
With a small rubber ball
And Lincoln Logs for pins
Set up at the end of a hall
In my grandparents' apartment.

Growing up I celebrated
Five of my birthdays
At a bowling alley in LA
As my love for bowling grew
Before I reached two digits
I began taking lessons with
A coach. I begged my parents
To take me bowling every weekend.
My father bought me
Two bowling balls by Storm
And bowling shoes by Dexter.

During my adolescence
After my first tournament
I became a member of the
U. S. Bowling Congress. Improving
My game physically and mentally,
Averaging a score above 170,
I continued to practice my skills
Every Saturday afternoon,
Spare shooting, angling an approach
To the pocket, managing my knee bend,
And controlling ball speed.

Going to Pace University in NYC
I found a bowling alley
Off the F train at Avenue X
In Brooklyn where I continued
To practice every Saturday
Except during finals.

By the time I make my living
I plan to bowl in many leagues
And tournaments. The game
Builds in me the ability to be
Patient and to trust my instincts.
It keeps me in the moment.

College

Pace University was the first of four colleges to accept me
Chose Pace as my learning home
Felt oriented on a boat-ride
Studied Political Science and Social Justice
Wanted more than just a good experience

Freshman Year
Joined a first year intensive program
Developed time management strategies

Sophomore Year
Discussed presidential debates
Taught democracy and human rights
Volunteered with New York Cares: painted a school and cleaned
benches
Attended my first Model UN conference in New York
Participated in my first employment readiness workshop
Interned at Partners for Progressive Israel

Junior Year

Featured in magazines and online websites
Rebuilt damaged homes in Rockaway Beach
Attended my second Model UN conference in New York
Became a member of honorary organizations

Spoke in a panel and wrote an Op Ed
Won an award for my contributions

Senior Year

Conducted a study on quality education for students with autism
Attended my last Model UN conference, in Italy
Participated in my last employment readiness workshop

Received comprehensive support all four years
Graduated with honors
Dedicated this victory to loved ones
Pace University took me on an incredible journey

I have been a student in many cultures

Discovered the American Institute for Foreign Studies

Traveled to Quito, Ecuador January 2017
Studied Geological and Environmental Relations
Lived with a Host Family in San Cristobal
Practiced Spanish everyday
Looked at pottery and reached the equator

Traveled to Barcelona, Spain Fall 2017
Studied Global Politics and Euro-Mediterranean Relations
Blogged my ventures on the website
Took excursions to Andalucia, Pyrenees, and Morocco
Cooked sauced breads and tortillas

Wanted to travel further
Researched hostels in The Czech Republic and Hungary
Joined European touring groups
Explored art museums, old synagogues, and churches
Walked across bridges in Prague
Soaked in warm tubs in Budapest

Traveled to Berlin, Germany January 2019

Studied the Rise of Anti-Semitism

Visited palaces, museums, and concentration camps

Took an excursion to Warsaw, Poland

Controlled my emotions with the genocide of European Jews

Learned to be mindful

Global Practices

Stumbled upon a 300 Level Poli-Sci course
Model United Nations

Took the class for three semesters
Researched and wrote a position paper
Learned UN documentation

2017 National Model United Nations Conference-NY
Represented Iraq in
High Level Political Forum and Sustainable Development
Drafted a resolution on educational needs, decent work, and
technology
Team won an honorable mention delegation award

2018 National Model United Nations Conference-NY
Applied and chose to take on a committee role
Became the Rapporteur for the International Organization of
Migration
Assisted committee directors with edits on submitted draft
resolutions
Team won multiple team honorable mention delegation awards

Summer 2018, found a Global Studies program at the Graduate Institute of Geneva

Traveled to Switzerland to explore the establishment of the UN

Visited several United Nations agencies

Represented Uganda in a Human Rights Council simulation

Discussed a resolution written by the General Assembly on ending poverty

2019 International Model United Nations conference in Rome

Represented China in

The Economic and Social Council

Drafted a resolution on water sanitations and

Protection of indigenous people

Team won a diplomacy award

Enhanced my advocating skills

Made friendships, and practiced global negotiation

Sense of Direction

In Washington DC
Learning the cities public transportation
Want to go to the Washington Monument from Union Station
Pull out my map, read the route
Board the metro on the red line

Transfer at Metro Center
Take the orange, or blue line to Smithsonian
Walk for nine to ten minutes
Arrive at my destination
Explore the landmark around the flags

Feel a little tired after a good exercise
Ready to go back to the hotel and get some rest
Want to go to the Crystal Gateway Marriot from the Monument
Notice that the blue line is out of service
Get in touch with my imaginary compass

Visualize another route
Walk to L'Enfant Plaza and
Take the yellow line to Crystal City
Enter the hotel Marriot
Fall into bed

The Black Mamba

Three championships wearing number 8
Two championships wearing number 24 with NBA Finals MVP
Two Olympic Gold Medals one in 2008 and one in 2012
Eighteen All Star Games with four MVPs

A legend
Kobe Bryant spoke at after school programs
Founded the *Kobe Bryant China Fund*
Won an Oscar for *Dear Basketball*
Became a best-selling author for
Mamba Mentality, How I play the game

So stunned when I discovered your biggest mistakes
You admitted and learned from those errors
The forgivable assault that is still questioned
The slur that resulted in a $100,000 fine

Your determination showed you were a tireless competitor
Your legendary success will always outmaneuver the flaws
When you fell in the helicopter crash
My face was wet

Emotion was expressed in many ways from the fans and myself
Games begun with an 8 or 24 second violation
Flowers, candles, gear and a writing wall in Downtown LA
Graffiti all over the city of Angels
I obtained number 24 on my cap

I created a poster of your wisdom
I listened to your message *"Love what you do."*

Rest In Peace
My biggest inspiration, favorite athlete, and true hero

Intend Connect Attain

I visualized a puzzle of 500 pieces
I was surrounded by kids like me
I sat on the grass
I contemplated strategies to express myself

I wanted to match the pieces together
I presented my autism speech
I got outstanding remarks and gave countless hugs
I asked questions to learn about the friends I was making

I solved the puzzle
I learned to listen
I bonded with amazing friends from all over the world
I have more puzzles to solve

Overcoming

"I love it when people doubt me. It makes me work harder to prove them wrong." – Derek Jeter

They viewed me in a cruel and envious way
I kept being myself

They said I brag about my success
I was honored to share my accomplishments

They triggered my attachments to sports and favorite athletes
I practiced everyday with coaches myself and won championships

They bad-mouthed my world travels
I felt motivated to keep blazing new trails

They said I only like movies that settle in the city that never sleeps
I was grateful for The Incredibles and Star Wars

They told me summer camp is not for me
I found a home away from home and matured

They called me obsessive when I expressed my love for NYC
I was the first student from my school to apply
And get into universities out of state

They disrespected my academic performance
I became the valedictorian of my high school graduating class

They disclosed that college in New York
Would never amount to anything for me
I am a Magna Cum Laude BA graduate of Pace University

Their negativity fueled me to use
My determination